THE HIDDEN POWER OF WORDS

Words That Empower

Dorothea Smothermon

DS Publishing   Fallbrook   California

DS Publishing
P.O. Box 422
Fallbrook, CA 92088-0422

This book was published in Canada as an electronic book in 2014, ISBN 978-0-25922-1.

Cover design by Mark at Genco Printers, Fallbrook, California.

ISBN 978-0-692-27383-8

I want to thank Drude Clark and Reba Lemmons for their invaluable support, encouragement, and critical reading. They are dear friends and fellow travelers on the path to self-improvement and enlightenment who accompanied me on this writing journey from beginning to end.

TABLE OF CONTENTS

INTRODUCTION

I met Lori Rekowski when she moved to the apartment complex that I manage. A friendship developed immediately, which was unusual because I tend to keep some distance between myself and tenants. In the process of getting acquainted, Lori mentioned her book <u>A Victim No More</u>. She briefly described what it was about and some of the tools she used to break away from the pain and abuse she had encountered throughout her life.

In our conversations, I realized Lori was using a number of words that were negative in connotation, so we began to talk about the energy created by some of the words she was using and how it affected her. It was at that time that Lori began to tell me I had to write a book about the power of words so that others could be helped with this tool as well. I focused on the victim consciousness to illustrate the power of words that we hear and say. Even though this book is written from the victim perspective, it has a broad application. We all need to monitor our words and thoughts.

The Edgar Cayce material helped me to see the damage that negative thoughts and words can cause and I was able to change from a person who spent more time in a negative frame of mind than in a positive one. As I studied the Cayce information, there were a number of one-liners that grabbed my attention. One of them related to the study of the deeper meaning of numbers. At that time, I had been playing with numerology and finding it a useful tool to understand people, especially my family. Over the years, certain words would catch my attention and I would wonder what the real impact of the word was. I began to apply numerology to words and found it very fascinating. I realized that by using numerology, I could get a better perspective of the energy of the word in question. Then I began to include a section on the deeper meaning of words in the traditional numerology workshops I conducted.

The idea that knowledge not used is sinful or selfish is another one-liner that caused me to stop and think. Since I spent a fair amount of time working with numerology, I began to look for better ways to use that information.

I decided that since like attracts like, I want to be more careful of what I attract into my life by making better choices with the words I use. I also realize that if I truly want to be of service, I need to share this information.

THE POWER OF WORDS

Every word carries an idea, and the character of that idea can either be constructive or destructive. The Metaphysical Bible Dictionary says words are made active in the body through their being received in the mind and carried into the body through the sub-consciousness of one's thought. The Edgar Cayce material, as well as other sources, indicates that thoughts are things; they can become crimes or miracles, damaging or inspiring, depending on the intent of the thinker.

If you read the Holy Bible, you will find the first chapter of the first book tells of God's desire to create the heavens and the earth. Each thing was brought into being by God saying "Let there be light …," "Let there be a firmament…" etc. John begins his gospel in the New Testament with "In the beginning was the Word, and the Word was with God, and the Word was God," which also shows the powerfully creative aspect of words by relating them to God. It is a very subtle presentation of the concept of the creativity of words. Another source relating the power of thought and words is found in Deepak Chopra's book The Seven Spiritual Laws of Success. He presents the Law of Intention and Desire which is based on the fact that energy and information exist everywhere. Intention and desire are the organizing tools which we use to form our reality. The idea that we can change things by changing our thoughts takes some getting used to. If we make a mistake it doesn't have to affect us forever; change your thoughts and watch what happens.

The movie "What Dreams May Come" starring Robin Williams, based on a book by Richard Matheson with the same title, clearly shows the creative power of thought. In this movie the place people find themselves after death reflects what was important to them before they died. When the character played by Williams died, he found himself in an area exactly like a painting hanging in his living room that was dear to him because it was painted by his wife. And when his daughter in the film died, she built an area that was exactly like the place depicted in the painting that was on her bedroom wall.

I have had some personal experience with the creative power of thought. At one point in my life, I decided I wanted yellow canna lilies in my yard. Most people would just go to the store and buy them, but not me. I was a real estate broker at the time and the realtors would go see the new listings each week. I knew I would see a lot of yards and so I looked for the flowers each week for several weeks. My idea was that I would offer to help clear out the excess canna and ask if I could have what was removed from the flower beds. Then I forgot about my quest.

After some time had passed, I noticed a pencil-like "weed" that had come up at the trunk of a forty year old avocado tree which was visible through the window over my computer. As time passed, I watched the plant get taller, yet still pencil-like. Soon a leaf began to unfold and I decided it was one of the white calla lilies that grew so profusely in my yard and grove. However, that was not the case. When the leaf was fully unfolded, it was not shaped like a calla lily leaf. When the flower shoot emerged and opened, I realized it was the yellow canna I wanted. At that point, I had lived on the property for five years. The plant was not there when we bought the place, and no one in their right mind would put canna at the base of an avocado tree. It was a thought provoking experience.

Since I was a student of the Edgar Cayce material, I came to realize my focused desire for the canna had manifested the plant and it was in the perfect location for me to see daily. I also manifested yellow tulips and good parking places in jammed parking lots just to test the theory.

Richard Bach also talks about the power of thought when he mentions vaporizing clouds in his book <u>Illusions,</u> so I tried my hand at that and had some success. As I focused on a small, fairly thick cloud, it disappeared while others beside it did not. It was at that point that I began to realize we have no idea of the power of thoughts and words.

Words begin in the mind, where they can be left as a thought or given voice. Thought affects the body just as spoken words do. Healing, when the recipient is not present, can be done by the power of the spoken word and/or the power of thought. Specific words remind the subconscious that it can change the vibrations of the body and bring about balance and, ultimately, healing. The subconscious mind does not have a truth filter, thus when ideas are submitted to the subconscious mind it believes what is presented. It takes the conscious mind to determine if the idea is valid, truthful, or helpful by relating it to the current belief system of the person. If the idea fits, it is accepted as truth.

Every word or thought fosters either status quo or change. Thoughts and spoken words communicate messages to the subconscious mind where the building process begins. When the message is constructive, a positive pattern develops. As the building proceeds, the universe begins to restructure or reorder events in your life. When the message is not constructive, positive patterns are torn down, eaten away, and replaced with negative patterns. The negative patterns attract negative events whereas the positive patterns attract positive events. The patterns become magnets, which is a demonstration of the universal law of 'Like Attracts Like' which is presented in Bruce McArthur's book <u>Your Life and Why It Is the Way It Is</u>. The old adage "birds of a feather flock together…" comes to mind bearing out the magnetic aspect of thoughts and actions. You tend to be more comfortable with those who think and act the way you do, because their attitudes and actions fit with what you think are acceptable, thereby fitting into your belief system.

Both silent and verbalized words create attitudes, and in turn attitudes create emotions which impact actions. You read a person's thoughts partly by their body language and partly by their attitudes. Facial expressions have long been the measure of thoughts. If you watch as someone receives a compliment, you notice a change in the expression on their face, usually a smile or other positive change. By the same token, a derogatory comment usually brings a less than positive reaction. The energy of the words is internalized and begins to affect the cells in the body.

In his book, The Hidden Message of Water, Dr. Masaru Emoto proves the effect of words on water crystals by photographing the crystals before and after the water was subjected to a word or thought. Positive words produced beautiful, harmonious crystals whereas words of destruction and hate produced ugly unbalanced crystals. Since the human body ranges from 57 to 75 percent water, you can see how the body can be affected.

"What the Bleep Do We Know!?" is a movie that deals with this concept. There is a scene where the actress, Marlee Matlin, responds to this idea by actually drawing hearts and positive phrases all over her body. The movie challenges us to answer the question of why we repeatedly take the same jobs, choose the same type of partners, and go to the same places. The answer to these questions boils down to the fact that if we do not change our thoughts or we allow others to do our thinking for us, as victims often do, the same reality keeps repeating itself and situations remain the same.

Victims buy into the abuser's statement "If you had been good, I wouldn't have to punish you." This punishment for bad behavior is presented to almost everyone very early in life. Many parents use this concept as they raise their children. "No" is usually the first directive a child hears in the early years of life. Various forms of punishment are used to teach the child proper behavior and it is billed as an act of love. Because parents love their children and don't want them hurt, it becomes necessary to change a child's behavior when safety issues are involved.

What starts out constructive many times is overdone and becomes a cruelty. It is no wonder some people submit to those same painful experiences later in life. They believe the painful acts will stop at some point because eventually their parent had stopped using the painful mode of parenting and ultimately the behavior change was a good thing. Or they are conditioned to believe that abuse is an aspect of love. If you find yourself in this scenario, as the situation escalates, you will feel trapped and/or rationalize the experience as being deserved. The longer the situation continues, the harder it is to break free. The more difficult it is to evaluate the situation accurately, the harder it becomes to set or enforce boundaries. Your protective shell takes a beating and begins to crumble. You question your judgment and your ability to make good choices because you are constantly told you are wrong by the very people who should love and protect you. You want these people who are hurting you to admire you, to be proud of you, to love you and ultimately to change the way they treat you. Guilt, a very powerful emotion, begins to surface.

Low self-esteem and tunnel vision are a part of guilt. As a victim, you are crushed by a repeated bombardment of negative, painful experiences. Self-worth becomes non-existent and bitterness takes hold of your mind. Your focus collapses and you begin to sabotage yourself by closing in on yourself and refusing to look for alternatives. The belief that you are not worth the effort causes you to refuse to participate in activities that could be healing. You believe it is a waste of time to try something different. You believe no one cares anymore and life just is not worth living, which can lead to suicidal thoughts.

A serious consequence of guilt is the difficulty encountered when setting boundaries. Boundaries are part of your protective shell. Boundaries set the actions and thoughts you will claim as your own and what you will tolerate from others. They act as a first line of defense, a sort of barrier to unwanted thoughts and actions. When there are no boundaries or very flexible boundaries, it is too easy to allow others to have control over your value system. You question your own judgment and let someone else influence your actions and thoughts. You find yourself going along with the program regardless of the author. You begin to lose your perspective of self and your expectations. As you are continually being subjected to painful experiences, trust is ripped from you and it is difficult to trust anyone again.

Another aspect of guilt is shame. Shame is a destructive emotion that has long been used to change behavior. It also starts early in life. Shame is another tool parents use to teach acceptable behavior. "Shame on you" and "What will people think?" are statements we hear in the maturation process. Again what starts out as beneficial can become cruel. A sense that you must "suffer the consequences" sets in and begins to control your mind. And the vicious circle starts again. You, as the victim, are labeled as defective, of little value and are treated as such. Your self-worth takes a dive and the pain increases. A feeling of hopelessness and powerlessness overcomes you, again sometimes prompting suicidal thoughts and even suicidal actions.

Then blame, also an aspect of guilt, enters the picture. Blame is a double edged sword. Self-blame fosters the idea of guilt and all the destructive reactions that follow. If you have in fact done something wrong, shame is a powerful incentive to change that behavior. If not, you internalize the emotion along with its paralyzing, negative impact. Putting the blame on others is just as damaging, because it passes control to others, thereby making it almost impossible to envision change. There is a desire to just curl up and wish the world would go away. It seems useless to make an effort to do anything. The desire for being treated differently soon fades and hopelessness overshadows everything. You lose trust even in yourself. You lose your sense of safety. The ability to respond to what is going on in the present is negligible. There is no desire to seek changes and no desire to survive. Soon the wish to end it all can become uppermost in your mind.

Change begins in the mind and when the mind is overloaded, it's difficult to conceive of and build new constructive thought patterns. "Mind is the builder" is a concept found in many metaphysical philosophies. The book <u>The Power of Positive Thinking</u> by Norman Vincent Peale has been around for a long time. Here are some interesting ideas he presents in his work. "Reality is the mirror of your thoughts. Choose well what you put in front of the mirror." "Positive thinking is expecting, talking, believing, and visualizing what you want to achieve. It is seeing what you want as an accomplished fact." "To think negatively is like taking a weakening drug." "Being positive or negative are habits of thoughts that have a very strong influence on everyone's life."

Habits create automatic responses to events. Reaction, rather than action, becomes the normal response. The problem with reaction is that you don't react to what is going on currently. You are propelled back to the first time you were involved in a similar experience and replay the shock and pain of that episode. That original hurt and helplessness resurfaces and controls the mind. Repeated patterns create habits and habits create automatic behavior. You are like the hamster in the cage going round and round repeating the same actions again and again.

Breaking habits, especially the habit of negative thinking, takes focused effort which usually requires help from someone outside the situation. You need someone else to convince you that things can change, that you can get to a better place. Often you don't realize what you are doing and why you are doing it. You can't change something until you realize you are doing it and decide you want to act differently. You also need to know when you have slipped back into the old pattern. Many times you isolate yourself in an effort to keep the abuser from lashing out again, thereby making it more difficult to reach out for help.

To begin the healing process, a new filtering system must be applied. The first step to change is the re-evaluation of the mind. What habits have become entrenched? What reactions are automatic? Of what are you really guilty? How can you change your thinking? Who can you really trust? In the process of becoming healthy, the thought that others can be trusted to have your best interests at heart has to be planted in the mind and nurtured. In the beginning others have to be relied upon to help you evaluate the situation. Others have to be allowed to help you set new boundaries, new standards that aid the healing process. To change the situation and bring about healing, the mind has to be fed positive ideas continually.

Since guilt is the failure to live up to a standard, the standard not met must be examined. Whose standard is it? Is it your own standard or does it belong to someone else? Are you allowing others to control your thoughts and actions by using their standards? Are you blindly following others without thinking? Abiding by others' standards also begins early in life. First, your parents set standards for you. You found acceptable behavior brought positive responses. When you got to school, teachers and school officials set more standards, again teaching that behavior brings a reaction. Any law is another standard set by others that brings consequences when violated. Living by others' standards is a natural process of becoming an adult. Here again, what starts out as a positive, constructive activity can become toxic. When you get clear on the standards to which you choose to be held, the feeling of guilt will begin to fade. You are able to change what needs to be changed. Then a more positive thought pattern can take hold and begin to reorder the events that come to you.

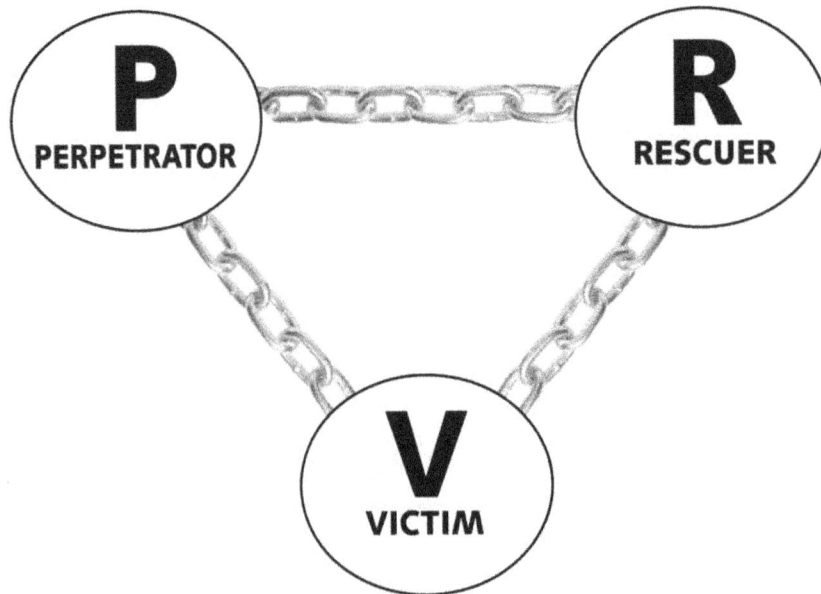

Painful Triangle

Figure 1

THE PAINFUL TRIANGLE

Let's look at various components that make up the drama surrounding the victim and the part words play. There are three major roles acted out in this arena: the perpetrator, the rescuer, and the victim. Stephen B. Karpman, M.D. uses the Karpman Drama Triangle to illustrate the toxic interplay of the persecutor, the rescuer and the victim. The persecutor or perpetrator is the controller, or the person in the position of power, which resonates to the negative aspect of power. The rescuer is the enabler, justifier or savior who exhibits the negative aspects of the mediator. The victim is the result of the negative treatment from the other two characters with reactions that resonate with the negative aspects of self-image. These roles are linked together, each with their own reaction to the negative aspects of power, and form a painful triangle that is very strong. (See Figure 1). And oddly enough the victim takes on each of these roles at one time or another in an effort to gain some control in their lives.

The victim first experiences the role of perpetrator through other people. The payback of this role is power and control. The perpetrator unleashes a painful accusation or comment or even a physical abuse that is shocking. The normal protective shell we all have is bombarded and closes in on the victim, which can make a productive response to the perpetrator very difficult. The vocabulary of the perpetrator includes words like punish, suffer, guilt, shame, blame, ignorant, useless, and unlovable. These words all carry ideas that are negative in character, meaning these words are criminal when intentionally directed at someone. Any attempt by the victim for self-protection is met with promises of retaliation from the perpetrator. The threat of the perpetrator to hunt down and punish the victim, should they try to leave the situation, is continually present. Even though the perpetrator may promise to stop the damaging acts the promise is eventually broken. Since there were no repercussions for previous bad behavior, other blows are delivered, usually in a cyclic pattern.

Another role is the rescuer who attempts to fix everything instead of allowing the victim to solve the problem. The payback for the rescuer includes social acceptability, being seen as the good guy and being in control. Admittedly, as painful experiences continue and worsen, the victim becomes less and less able to find solutions and looks to anyone who can fix the situation. Many times it creates a dependency on the rescuer. However, the solution presented by the rescuer does not include stopping the perpetrator nor does it help the victim break out of the victim role. Instead, on some occasions, there may be an attempt of the rescuer to rationalize the perpetrator's actions by finding plausible reasons for the abuse. There may be the misguided idea that the bad behavior is an aspect of love. In these situations, the rescuer minimizes the perpetrator's actions and encourages the victim to be patient and understanding with the perpetrator, when in fact, there is no way to understand intentional devastating acts as being acceptable for any reason. In most situations, the rescuer simply wants to remove the victim from the scene only to control the subsequent situation and at times become the new perpetrator. While the vocabulary of the rescuer is not as damaging as the perpetrator's, the attitude certainly is. The fact that there is a rescuer role is evidence of the victim's gullibility and the damage that has been done to their thought processes by the vicious triangle.

The third major role is that of the victim, the recipient of the violating verbiage and actions. In the beginning you, as the victim, look for an explanation of the perpetrator's behavior because you think it is impossible that someone who professes to love you can actually do such a thing. Your first thought is that you were mistaken and the perpetrator didn't really mean any harm. You then try to forgive and forget which would be possible if that was the only occurrence of the pain. However, the perpetrator does repeat the hurtful behavior. Each time, your protective shell is invaded a little more and you withdraw from interacting with others. When you, the victim, begin to act as the perpetrator, you turn inward and direct the destruction on yourself. In both roles there is the idea of deserving the pain, which leaves no room for hope or change. You may also inflict pain on others. When you, the victim, play the role of rescuer, it does not enter your mind that the painful behavior of the perpetrator is unacceptable. Also, you may focus all of your energy on other victims' problems and try to fix them at all costs. As the pain of the situation escalates, the futility of it weighs heavily on you and soon the desire or hope for change is non-existent. Then the wish or decision to end it all can become uppermost in your mind. Many victims attempt and some succeed in committing suicide because they have lost hope.

"Why do victims stay in the painful environment?" one might ask. Usually there is some kind of perk for staying. Possible paybacks for the victim may be getting attention, even negative attention, and not having to do certain tasks for which they are normally responsible. However, if the situation has gone on long enough the victim begins to believe that this is what they deserve and they cannot find a better life situation. They believe everyone will treat them the same way. In some situations the perpetrator may show some remorse for their behavior with empty promises, gifts and shows of affection, which can also be mistakenly seen as a payback or perk.

A SURPRISING TOOL

Now it's time to consider the concepts that the mind is the builder and thoughts and words are either crimes or miracles. Even the possibility that these concepts could be true makes it imperative that we pay attention to the words we use and/or take to heart. We need to examine more closely the deeper meaning of words if we want to change our experiences. With this idea in mind, I turned to the science of numbers which is also known as numerology. In this system, letters are assigned a numerical value. By converting the letters to numbers and arriving at a numerical value of a name, the hidden meaning or power of the name is revealed. Potential strengths and weaknesses become apparent and you can begin to work with the information to create a more balanced and less stressful experience for the individual.

Each number has a related color, musical note, and gemstone. You will find working with the related energies makes some events more bearable, more understandable. You begin to see the value of an experience as a learning opportunity instead of a bruising episode. I have analyzed the names of my family, friends, and others who would give me the name on their birth certificate. Many people tell me they are still using the colors and gemstones I had recommended, sometimes years earlier, because they were so helpful. The recommendations were based on the numerological information found in their name.

The vowels of a name reveal the soul's urge or heart's desire or the true inner strength of an individual. The consonants reveal the outer personality or how the individual deals with others. Together, all of the letters of a name reveal the destiny or the expression of the individual. I had been working with names for over ten years when I wondered what would happen if I worked with words the way I worked with names. Needless to say, I was astounded by the outcome. I found the hidden meanings are right on with the general idea carried in the word. It occurred to me that I needed alternate terms that would relate to words. I replaced the term *inner strength* (vowels) with the term *essence*. I changed the term *outer personality* (consonants) to the term *channel* which reveals how the essence is manifested. The *expression* (all letters) became the *message* showing what the subconscious hears when the word is used.

For instance, the essence, which is revealed by the vowels, of the word LOVE is 11. That means it is enlightening and testing. The consonants of LOVE add up to 7 which reveals that the channel through which the enlightenment happens is going within and trusting your inner knowledge. All the letters of LOVE add up to 9, which reveal the message of completions and healing being communicated to the subconscious mind. Think of the love relationships you have encountered with parents, friends, lovers, and your children. You will see all of the above mentioned aspects in the difficulties, the learning, and the healing or ending of relationships. The word WORK is also interesting. Its essence is a 6 which means taking responsibility for self and being of service. The channel through which the essence is accomplished is a 7 which means trusting your own knowledge. The message received by the subconscious is 4 or hard work, self-discipline and organization. How can you better describe work? When you go to work you take responsibility for the tasks required of you. We all know that self-discipline is necessary to stay employed and organization is necessary to accomplish all the tasks that need to be done.

I use numerology with the alternate terms as a tool when I want to look at the deeper meaning of words. How does it work? In one system of numerology, letters are given a value based on their position in the alphabet. That is, the value of A is 1 because it is the first letter and

B is 2 because it is the second letter and so on through the alphabet. There are other numerology systems but this one gives me more useful information about the strengths and weaknesses of individuals, as well as the deeper meaning, the energy, of words.

An easy way to find the value of the letters is to set up a chart using the numbers of 1 to 9. Place the letters of the alphabet under the numbers. A is the first letter, J is the tenth letter, and S is the nineteenth letter. They would all be listed below the 1. B, K, and T would be placed below the 2. C, L, and U go below the 3 and so on. (See Chart A below.) Once this is set up you can begin to work with words or names. Collect the vowels and consonants separately. Y is the only letter that can be either vowel or consonant. Basically, if "y" sounds like another vowel when you say the word, use it as a vowel. If in doubt, try using it both ways. One will be more consistent with the general idea of the word. Add the values of the vowels until you get a single digit or a master number of 11, 22, 33, or 44. Add the values of the consonants and then all the letters in the word until you arrive at three separate numbers. (See Chart B below.) Find the meanings of the numbers that follow below and see what the hidden power of the word is. See how the word impacts you.

Chart A

VALUE	1	2	3	4	5	6	7	8	9
LETTERS	A	B	C	D	E	F	G	H	I
	J	K	L	M	N	O	P	Q	R
	S	T	U	V	W	X	Y	Z	

Chart B

WORD	L	O	V	E		
VOWELS		6		5	6+5=11	ESSENCE IS 11
CONSONANTS	3		4		3+4=7	CHANNEL IS 7
ALL LETTERS	3	6	4	5	3+6+4+5=18 1+8=9	MESSAGE IS 9

ESSENCE = VOWELS   CHANNEL = CONSONANTS   MESSAGE = ALL LETTERS

In this science, numbers are added together to get a single digit, except repeating digits such as 11, 22, 33 and 44. These are considered master numbers and are not added further unless you are determining the value of the letter. In other words, the value of J is 1 because it is the 10th letter and 1 plus 0 is 1. S is 1 because it is the 19th letter and 1 plus 9 is 10 which in turn 1 plus 0 is 1. K, the 11th letter, is placed under the 2 because 1 plus 1 is 2 and V is the 22nd letter and is placed under the 4 because 2 plus 2 is 4.

Let's look at some key words and other components associated with the different numbers. Some of the meanings ascribed to ONE are new beginnings, inventiveness, leadership, aggressiveness, and independence. The negative aspects of ONE are having no control, or forcing one's will regardless, or becoming too dependent on others, or abusing leadership. The color associated with ONE is red. Red is a color that builds red blood cells, increases blood circulation, and warms the body. Red has become linked to Christmas and Valentine's Day, both of which are related to the heart and love. Red has also been associated with the negative emotion of anger. I'm sure you know the term "seeing red" is used to imply anger and rage. And the phrase "hot under the collar" is also used to describe someone who is angry. Ruby and red garnet both have the same vibratory rate of ONE, as does the musical note 'C'. Wearing the color or gemstones, thinking of red, or hearing the musical note 'C' are subtle ways of bringing the ONE energy to the subconscious mind and the body to create change.

The number TWO is associated with orange, moonstone, and the musical note 'D'. Adaptable, tactful, understanding, cautious, and gentle describe the energy of TWO. Also the capability of time management, cooperation, and the ability to settle disputes are associated with the TWO. The negative TWO can be tactless and dictatorial, as well as argumentative, willful and uncooperative. Moonstone, regardless of its color, has a gentle impact on the emotions, thereby having a calming effect. If you do not like to wear orange, use orange accents in your home or listen to the musical note 'D' to supply the needed energy to the body and mind. Orange food is also a good way to get the color into your vibratory system.

THREE means expressing the joy of living and self-expression as well as being dramatic, communicative, and creative. A sunny yellow, yellow topaz and the musical note 'E' all have the vibratory rate of THREE. Yellow citrine also works from the color standpoint. The negative aspects of THREE are conceit and arrogance, over-confidence or lacking self-confidence. The phrase "being yellow bellied" indicates cowardliness, having no backbone or confidence. In the real estate market, we found homes painted a soft yellow or having yards with yellow flowers sold more quickly.

FOUR is about stability, hard work, self-discipline, organization, practicality and endurance. The color green, emeralds, green jade, and the musical note 'F' have the same vibratory rate as the FOUR. Not following orders, being scatter-brained and harboring jealousy are all associated with the dark side of the FOUR. You may have heard the term "green-eyed monster" or "green with envy." Both are negative in connotation. When I was in school, there were consequences for not wearing green on St. Patrick's Day. The positive aspect of green is associated with healing and it is also associated with Christmas.

Freedom and change are major definitions of FIVE. It is versatile, resourceful, active, sensuous, and adventurous. Blue is the color of FIVE and the gemstones are aquamarine and turquoise. Musical note 'G' has the same vibrations as FIVE. The negative side of FIVE is associated with depression, forced limits, addiction to sensation and resistance to change. "Blue Monday" and "being blue" are terms reflecting depression and lack of freedom or lack of specific company. Elvis Presley sang a song about "Blue Suede Shoes" implying the specialness and resourcefulness and the movement aspect of blue. The song warned others to be careful of his blue suede shoes.

SIX is described as service, family, responsibility, and counselor. Indigo, natural pearls, and the musical note 'A' all vibrate to the SIX energy. SIX wants to bring peace and harmony, truth and integrity to its space. Some numerologists believe a person who is in a 6 personal year will have wedding bells ringing for them that year. The negative aspect of SIX is being an enabler, being a slave, and being unable to work together in relationships.

The SEVEN looks for answers. It is self-image, introspection and intuition. SEVENS trust their inner knowledge. SEVENS need some alone time. The negative aspect of SEVEN expresses gloom, disappointment, lack of self-protection, and poor self-image. Violet, amethyst and the musical note 'B' all relate to the energy of SEVEN.

EIGHT will take over. It is power seeking, controlling, strong-willed, and ambitious. The negative aspect of EIGHT is ruthlessness, total domination, and greed. Pink, pink quartz, diamond, and the musical note High 'C' all have the energy of EIGHT. The custom of using diamonds in engagement rings shows the subtle understanding of the changes for a woman when she marries. She must control the activities inside her home. With her new status, a whole different set of skills is needed to run a household and have a family, especially if she also works outside of the home.

Compassion and selflessness describe the NINE. Universality, patience, tolerance, completions, healing, and selfless service are qualities of the NINE. The negative expression of NINE is illness, self-serving and insensitivity. NINE impacts large numbers of people. All colors of the rainbow, or white, when the colors are in balance relate to NINE. Opal and musical note High 'D' also have the same vibration as the number NINE.

The master number ELEVEN is described as enlightening, altruistic, courageous, and strong in leadership, all of which can cause testing. It is a vibration that brings repeat experiences to test the ability to stay true to what is known. Negative aspects of the ELEVEN are being unfair, severe, prejudiced, and using power harmfully. Silver, mother of pearl, and musical note High 'E' all have the same vibratory rate as the ELEVEN.

Building success step by step, reaching goals and victory are the key words for the TWENTY-TWO, which is a master number also. Attainment of impossible dreams is possible with the TWENTY-TWO energy. The negative side of this energy is extremes, extravagance and overindulgence. Pink coral, luminous gold, and the musical note High 'F' all bear the energy of TWENTY-TWO.

THIRTY-THREE is another master number. It is the master teacher who is self-disciplined, discriminating, self-sacrificing, resourceful and imaginative. The negative expression of the THIRTY-THREE is emotional instability, being anxious and fearful, and sacrificing self for any cause whether or not it is a worthy cause. Luminous pale blue, Lapis Lazuli, and musical note High 'G' all have the same vibratory rate as the master number THIRTY-THREE.

FORTY-FOUR is a master decision maker whose decisions impact large numbers of people. They are steady workers who will persevere to reach their chosen goal. FORTY-FOUR prefers useful enterprises that are very resourceful. The negative expression of FORTY-FOUR is undisciplined, forcing issues, misuse of information from the intuitive sources.

One of the things your first name reveals when using numerology is the method you use to solve problems. It might be helpful for you to check your name. Let's use the name Anne as an example. Anne's problem-solving is done by taking responsibility through looking for a new way to reach the wisdom which allows her to find the solution. (See Chart C.) Now find your method of problem-solving using chart D.

Chart C

Word	A	N	N	E								Essence	6
Vowels	1			5						1+5=6		Essence	6
Consonants		5	5							5+5=10, 1+0=1		Channel	1
All Letters	1	5	5	5						1+5+5+5=16, 1+6=7		Message	7

Chart D

Word	(YOUR NAME)											
Vowels											Essence	
Consonants											Channel	
All Letters											Message	

There are many good numerology books that have a much broader description for each of these energies. If this has tickled your interest, you can learn more by reading <u>Numerology and the Devine Triangle</u> by Faith Javane and Dusty Bunker. This is one of my favorite numerology books because they have gone to great lengths to teach the in-depth significance of each of the numbers.

WORD	P	U	N	I	S	H							
VOWELS		3		9							3+9=12; 1+2=3	**ESSENCE IS**	**3**
CONSONANTS	7		5		1	8					7+5+1+8=21; 2+1=3	**CHANNEL IS**	**3**
ALL LETTERS	7	3	5	9	1	8					7+3+5+9+1+8=33	**MESSAGE IS**	**33**

Damaging Vocabulary

By "damaging vocabulary," I am referring to words with the hidden power to create devastating reactions. The message of a word is relayed to the subconscious mind, and subsequently to the soul, which starts a chain reaction, thereby creating a pattern. As the pattern is repeated, it is strengthened and eventually a habit is formed. Positive patterns create positive habits, just as negative patterns create negative habits. Consequently, thoughts and words are things that can become either crimes or miracles, can either tear down or build up. Unfortunately, all of this is done without you being conscious of the impact. You may be unaware of some of the habits created. Habits, even those you deliberately develop, create automatic reactions. Once an automatic reaction is developed, habits become difficult, but not impossible, to change.

Let's work with the word "punish." Generally when someone is punished, it is because they have done something wrong which warrants corrective behavior. Just hearing the word punish is unsettling. Then to follow up with punishing actions can be terrifying, especially if there is no misbehavior. Undeserved punishment causes bitterness, withdrawal, and confusion. It can damage your self-image. You begin to doubt your ability to make good decisions and use good judgment.

So what is the hidden power of the word PUNISH? Using numerology as a tool, we find both the essence (vowels) and the channel (consonants) of the word PUNISH are a 3; meaning it impacts self-confidence, joy, and creativity. Since the character of the idea carried in PUNISH is negative, the impact is negative or destructive. The message (all the letters) the subconscious hears is (33) a failure to protect. Again, since the character of the idea of PUNISH is negative, the impact is destructive, meaning you did not take the opportunity to protect and teach correctly.

WORD	C	O	N	T	R	O	L			
VOWELS		6				6		6+6=12, 1+2=3	ESSENCE IS	3
CONSONANTS	3		5	2	9		3	3+5+2+9+3=22	CHANNEL IS	22
ALL LETTERS	3	6	5	2	9	6	3	3+6+5+2+9+6+3=34, 3+4=7	MESSAGE IS	7

For the rescuer, the idea of punishment is downplayed or ignored in an effort to smooth things over. To the victim it is confusing, hurtful, and damaging. The victim tries unsuccessfully to understand what action caused the punishment. The dictionary defines punish as to cause suffering, and to chastise, both of which are negative in connotation, and that is what the perpetrator intends. Most of the perpetrator's interaction related to the victim is targeted to making the victim feel guilty, devalued, and helpless; the goal is to take the power from the victim. When the perpetrator repeatedly says to the victim "you shouldn't have done that / now look what you have done / you know better than to do that / you made me do it / [or] now you have to take your punishment," the stage is set for punishment. When you, the victim, are punished, it erodes your mind into thinking you have committed a gross error. You question your judgment and your critical thinking abilities. Self-confidence begins to be chipped away and a little bit of self is lost with each attack. The purpose of punishment is to gain control.

Control is another concept that must be dealt with early in life. Parents and teachers control most of the activities in which you are involved. Again something that starts out as beneficial can become harmful and degrading. CONTROL is defined as exercising power or limits and restrictions and is another word that impacts self-confidence and joy since the essence (vowels) of control is a 3. The channel (consonants) used is 22 which means building step by step. The message (all letters) is 7 which means trust your inner knowledge and/or to withdraw into a protective shell. The character of the idea of the word CONTROL is neither negative nor positive. The character changes with the way CONTROL is used. It is negative when the perpetrator establishes CONTROL over the victim, either physically and/or mentally. It is also negative when the rescuer succeeds in removing the victim

WORD	P	O	W	E	R							ESSENCE IS	11
VOWELS		6		5						6+5=11		ESSENCE IS	11
CONSONANTS	7		5		9					7+8+9=21, 2+1=3		CHANNEL IS	3
ALL LETTERS	7	6	5	5	9					7+6+5+5+9=32, 3+2=5		MESSAGE IS	5

WORD	E	M	P	O	W	E	R				ESSENCE IS	7
VOWELS	5			6		5				5+6+5=16, 1+6=7	ESSENCE IS	7
CONSONANTS		4	7		5		9			3+5+2+9+3=22	CHANNEL IS	22
ALL LETTERS	5	4	7	6	5	5	9			3+6+5+2+9+6+3=34, 3+4=7	MESSAGE IS	7

WORD	P	O	W	E	R	L	E	S	S		ESSENCE IS	7
VOWELS		6		5			5			6+5+5=16, 1+6=7	ESSENCE IS	7
CONSONANTS	7		5		9	3		1	1	7+5+9+3+1+1=26, 2+6=8	CHANNEL IS	8
ALL LETTERS	7	6	5	5	9	3	5	1	1	7+6+5+5+9+3+5+1+1=42, 4+2=6	MESSAGE IS	6

WORD	S	U	F	F	E	R					ESSENCE IS	8
VOWELS		3			5					3+5=8	ESSENCE IS	8
CONSONANTS	1		6	6		9				1+6+6+9=22	CHANNEL IS	22
ALL LETTERS	1	3	6	6	5	9				1+3+6+6+5+9=30, 3+0=3	MESSAGE IS	3

from the situation and later transfers control from the perpetrator to the rescuer. Loss of control makes the victim feel degraded, useless, and powerless.

POWER, which is defined as capacity, strength, and control, is another neutral word. The essence (11) of the word POWER is challenging and enlightening, using the channel (3) of confidence. The message (5) the subconscious hears is change or use all the five senses to gather information. Yet when you add the letters *e m* at the beginning you have the word EMPOWER, which changes everything. The character of the idea conveyed by the word EMPOWER is positive, the essence (7) is trust your inner knowledge through the channel (7) of self-image. The message (5) to the subconscious mind is change. When you add *less* to power, there is yet another change. The character of the idea transmitted by the word POWERLESS is negative. The essence (7) is low self-image, and distrust through the channel (8) of power and control. The message (6) is servant or slave. The perpetrator's power is evident when the victim is forced to submit to the perpetrator's words and actions without input in the decision-making process. This is very damaging to the victim. Power is also negative in the hands of the rescuer who wants to control the victim, believing the victim will be better off away from the perpetrator.

SUFFER is a word that has a negative connotation. The dictionary defines the word as feeling pain, undergoing something unpleasant, enduring something painful, or allowing something to happen. The essence (8) of SUFFER is misuse of power and control through (22) step by step action and the message (3) is destruction of joy and creativity. Again, since the character of the idea conveyed by the word SUFFER is negative, the impact is negative. All of the above meanings come into play in the statement "now you have to suffer the consequences."

WORD	A	T	T	A	C	K	E	D				
VOWELS	1			1			5			1+1+5=7	ESSENCE IS	7
CONSONANTS		2	2		3	2		4		2+2+3+2+4=13, 1+3=4	CHANNEL IS	4
ALL LETTERS	1	2	2	1	3	2	5	4		7+6+5+5+9=32, 3+2=5	MESSAGE IS	2

WORD	S	A	B	O	T	A	G	E			
VOWELS		1		6		1		5	1+6+1+5=13, 1+.=4	ESSENCE IS	4
CONSONANTS	1		2		2		7		1+2+2+7=12, 1+2=3	CHANNEL IS	3
ALL LETTERS	1	1	2	6	2	1	7	5	1+1+2+6+2+1+7+5=25, 2+5=7	MESSAGE IS	7

WORD	G	U	I	L	T						
VOWELS		3	9						3+9=12; 1+2=3	ESSENCE IS	3
CONSONANTS	7			3	2				7+3+2=12, 1+2=3	CHANNEL IS	3
ALL LETTERS	7	3	9	3	2				7+3+9+3+2=24, 2+4=6	MESSAGE IS	6

WORD	U	S	E	L	E	S	S				
VOWELS	3		5		5				3+5+5=13, 1+3=4	ESSENCE IS	4
CONSONANTS		1		3		1	1		1+3+1+1=6	CHANNEL IS	6
ALL LETTERS	3	1	5	3	5	1	1		3+1+5+3+5+1+1=19,1+9=10,1+0=1	MESSAGE IS	1

Another word that has a negative connotation is ATTACKED which is defined as harmed through violence or criticized. The essence (7) of attacked is poor self-image and inability to trust through the channel (4) of another's lack of self-discipline. The subconscious hears the message (2) imbalance, not cooperative, troublemaker. Attacks may be physical or verbal; both are equally damaging to the victim. Physical attacks require the body to heal. While verbal abuse is not visible, it can be just as devastating and more difficult to heal. ATTACKED is a word that is typically used by the victim to describe what has happened to them.

SABOTAGE, also negative in connotation, is used to describe the effects of abuse. It is defined as deliberate destruction and hindrance. Even though it is usually used by the victim, it still has the detrimental effects of reinforcing the situation being described. Its essence (4) is lack of discipline through (3) losing joy and enthusiasm. The message (7) communicated is untrustworthy, faulty perception.

GUILT is defined in one dictionary as the fact of having performed a wrong act, especially the violation of a law or a moral or ethical code. Another dictionary describes it as committing a specified or implied offense. It is interesting that punish and guilt have the same essence and channel, but a different message to communicate to the subconscious. The essence of GUILT is 3 which also impacts self-confidence and joy. The channel is a 3 which again deals with joy and confidence. The message is a 6 which communicates responsibility. Since GUILT has a negative connotation the impact is negative. Many times victims feel guilty when they try to take responsibility for others' actions. Guilt erodes joy and the victim begins to believe they are responsible for the situation.

USELESS is defined as unusable, unsuccessful or not able to do something properly. Not only is it a damaging word, it also is a negative feeling that destroys self-image when the victim is subjected to abuse. USELESS, negative in connotation, has an essence (4) of lack of discipline through service or servitude (6). The message (1) is difficulty in new beginnings, scattered, lack of the ability to find new answers, which is one of the reasons victims have difficulty in making the needed changes in their life

WORD	U	N	L	O	V	A	B	L	E			
VOWELS	3			6		1			5	3+6+1+5=15, 1+5=6	ESSENCE IS	6
CONSONANTS		5	3		4		2	3		5+3+4+2+3=17, 1+7=8	CHANNEL IS	8
ALL LETTERS	3	5	3	6	4	1	2	5	5	3+5+3+6+4+1+2+3+5=32, 3+2=5	MESSAGE IS	5

WORD	I	G	N	O	R	A	N	T			
VOWELS	9			6		1			9+6+1=16, 1+6=7	ESSENCE IS	7
CONSONANTS		7	5		9		5	2	7+5+9+5+2=28, 2+8=10, 1+0=1	CHANNEL IS	1
ALL LETTERS	9	7	5	6	9	1	5	2	9+7+5+6+9+1+5+2=44	MESSAGE IS	44

WORD	S	H	A	M	E						
VOWELS			1		5				1+5=6	ESSENCE IS	6
CONSONANTS	1	8		4					1+8+4=13, 1+3=4	CHANNEL IS	4
ALL LETTERS	1	8	1	4	5				1+8+1+4+5=19, 1+9=10, 1+0=1	MESSAGE IS	1

WORD	B	L	A	M	E						
VOWELS			1		5				1+5=6	ESSENCE IS	6
CONSONANTS	2	3		4					2+3+4=9	CHANNEL IS	9
ALL LETTERS	2	3	1	4	5				2+3+1+4+5=15, 1+5=6	MESSAGE IS	6

UNLOVABLE, defined as not deserving love, is also negative in connotation. The essence of the word is unsuccessful relationships (6) through misuse of power (8). The message is resisting change (5). You can see how detrimental the feeling is for the victim, and why the perpetrator would use the word. It helps to keep the status quo.

The definition of IGNORANT, another word used by the perpetrator, is lacking knowledge and being unaware. Negative in connotation, its essence (7) is lack of trusting inner knowledge. The channel (1) used is difficulty with new beginnings. Lack of common sense is the message (44) the subconscious hears when the word is used. It is another word that helps to keep things from changing.

SHAME is defined as a negative emotion, state of disgrace, or cause for regret, all of which are negative in connotation. The essence (6) of SHAME is negative aspects of responsibility and service which is accomplished through the channel (4) of discipline and hard work. The message (1) the subconscious mind hears is inability to do anything new and follow regardless of whom is leading.

BLAME is defined as being responsible for something wrong. It is also negative in connotation. Its essence (6) is the dark side of responsibility and service, which is accomplished through the channel (9) of compassionless intolerance. The message (6) the subconscious receives is placing responsibility whether or not it is deserved.

As you can see, all of these damaging words are used to keep the perpetrator in the position of power by controlling the situation, thereby keeping the victim downtrodden and submissive. The victim must adopt a new mindset. The victim must learn how to break this hold, to break the links that keep the vicious triangle intact. Then you, as the victim, can begin to climb back to self-respect and independence, to take back the control you have lost, and to find the peace necessary to live a productive life.

A WAY OUT

How can you make this tool work for you? The first step in breaking the chains of the painful triangle requires evaluation of all the characters of the triangle. Your own thoughts, words and actions, as a victim, can be just as damaging as the actions of the perpetrator or the rescuer. Are you using damaging words or thoughts? Do you replay the devastating experiences in your mind, thereby adding energy to the destruction? Do you automatically believe what the other characters of the triangle say without looking for their motive? Do you let the other two characters, perpetrator and rescuer, dominate your thinking and decision-making? When did you last make your own decisions? Do you realize that not making a decision is in fact a decision to continue the old pattern? When was the last time you set a boundary and held to it?

A time must come when you begin to challenge your thought process if change is ever going to happen because change begins in the mind. Thoughts have either positive or negative patterns that attract positive or negative events. Have you ever watched an interview on television of people who have just lost their home to fire? If you noticed, they usually say they had always been afraid something like that would happen. Self-fulfilling prophesy? An event given strength by their fear? Random loss? If you are what you think, be sure your thoughts are positive, loving, caring thoughts. Somewhere in the dark cloud there is a silver lining. It takes courage and persistence to find it. It takes focusing on what you really want rather than what you have experienced. Find ways to use this tool to create what you need, first in your mind and then the reality can follow. Are you ready to challenge the status quo? To make changes, you have to meet the challenge. You have to think. You have to believe. You have to act.

Speaking of change, change seems to be the biggest thing with which we all have to deal. Ultimately, every challenge seems to boil down to a change of one kind or another. CHANGE is a neutral word whose essence is responsibility through the channel of action. The message the subconscious hears is enlightenment. Albert Einstein said "No problem can be solved from the same level of consciousness that created it." In the book Illusions, Bach says "There is no such thing as a problem without a gift for you in its hands. You seek problems because you need their gifts." I believe we can gain access to the gifts by using the power of words and thoughts without having to always experience the pain.

One way to do this is replacing the damaging words with healing words. There is a difference between being abused and being punished. The difference is how you perceive the action. While the perpetrator will try to convince you that it was punishment, meaning that you deserved it, you have a choice in what you think of the situation. You can see it as punishment or as an opportunity for the perpetrator to change. You can remain a victim or you can begin to change the energy in the situation. If you can see that the perpetrator probably is not going to change, you can use your energy to find a different solution to the problem. You can begin to see each occurrence as an opportunity for the perpetrator and/or you to do something different. It is an opportunity to learn something about yourself and the perpetrator. The universe presents experiences that help you grow in knowledge and inner strength. You may discover you have had enough and begin to seek safe avenues of change. You will have to draw on your inner strength to follow through. As you begin to broaden your focus, you can see new opportunities, new ways to interact, new ways to get the help you need. The word OPPORTUNITY has a positive connotation and is defined as an advantageous chance or favorable conditions. The essence of the word is a 4 meaning self-discipline and organization through the channel (5) of taking action. The message (9) is healing and closure. In other words, make yourself take advantage of the situations that come up to do something different, to make things better. Since the change won't happen immediately, it will take some planning and some sticking with the new program to get to a new perspective.

Both control and power are neutral words. You need to find ways to focus on the positive aspects of these words. You can choose to control your thoughts. You can choose to control your actions instead of continuing to act out of habit. You can begin to gain some power with the choices you make. The meaning of CHOOSE is to decide from a range of options and/or make a deliberate decision. The essence of CHOOSE is 8 meaning power, even a higher power, through the channel of creativity. The message communicated to the subconscious is enlightening and testing. You will be tested with each new choice to see if you really want to change the situation. As you pass each test you can begin to see a new you. You emerge empowered.

There is a completely different impact in "suffer the consequences" versus "learn from the experience." While the essence of suffer is misuse of power, the essence of LEARN is take responsibility for your own thoughts and actions. The channel of suffer is step by step action, whereas the channel of learn is power. The message of suffer is destruction of joy and creativity, and the message of learn is change. When you replace the word *suffer* with the word *learn*, you are focusing on taking responsibility for your actions through positive use of power to create the needed change. While learn has a positive connotation and is healing, it sometimes feels negative because lessons can be painful. However, it usually takes some kind of pain to force the issue. If a challenge is not presented, the idea of change simply doesn't occur to you.

If you can see the perpetrator has proven his/her true colors again rather than thinking of being *attacked*, you can change your perception. If you fail to buy into the perpetrators idea of 'just rewards,' you can see the reality of the situation. It doesn't change the pain but it does change the impact of it. PROVEN is defined as tried and tested or shown to be true. Its essence is testing and enlightenment through trusting your inner knowledge to bring completion and healing. Even though you may believe you truly love the perpetrator, there is no aspect of love that allows for abuse. As the victim, a choice for healing may mean leaving the situation completely. Find the protection you need and stick to your choice. Beware of bargaining, empty promises, shows of affection, or gifts which are designed to regain control lost by the perpetrator.

You can replace the negative word *sabotage* with the more positive word *detour*. DETOUR means to deviate from a shorter, direct route or change from the expected. As you might guess, the essence of detour is change through the channel of serving a purpose thus conveying the message of enlightenment or testing. The purpose of a detour is to keep you out of harm's way. It may take longer to get where you are going, but you do eventually get there whereas sabotage just reinforces your faulty perception. If you can think of being detoured instead of sabotaged you can see that change is only delayed, not impossible.

The negative word *guilt* can be replaced with *non-judgment*. The purpose of guilt is to assign responsibility for actions. The negative impact of guilt causes you to accept responsibility for things others do instead of realizing the responsibility really belongs to someone else. NON-JUDGMENT, positive in connotation, does not consider responsibility. The essence of non-judgment is change through a higher level of love which brings enlightenment. It allows you to observe the situation without the hooks to drag you back into the vicious triangle. Non-judgment does not place the labels of right or wrong to an event. You are the only one who can accurately judge whether something is right or wrong for you, not the perpetrator, and not the rescuer. Being non-judgmental will allow you to get a clearer picture of the standards by which you are actually living. When you get clear on the standards you want to live by, a shift happens and a new response is possible, then the feeling of guilt begins to fade. You are able to change what needs to be changed. A more positive thought pattern can take hold and begin to reorder the events that come to you and the links holding you in the triangle begin to weaken.

Action can replace the negative word *useless* which is one of the harmful words used by the perpetrator. The message of useless is the inability to find new solutions. ACTION, on the other hand, has an essence of better self-concept through the channel of new beginnings to the message of empowerment. You begin to feel better about yourself if you actually do something to change the situation. Being productive creates new energy to continue the process.

Replace the word *unlovable* with the word *valuable* and watch what happens. If you are told you are unlovable, say to yourself that the speaker is entitled to an opinion but the truth of the matter is you are valuable. The essence of VALUABLE is new beginnings through the channel of creativity to bring order and peace. Another way to say it is that when you realize your own worth, you then have the motivation and the energy to create the necessary changes for a more peaceful lifestyle.

Being told you are *ignorant* should be met with your claiming your own *knowledge*. While the word ignorant is used to reduce your power, the word KNOWLEDGE is used to claim the ability to solve problems. The essence of knowledge is to trust your own inner wisdom through the channel of trusting your inner strength which allows you to bring about change. It is only when you know you can trust yourself and your decisions that you can make progress in changing what needs to be changed.

If you feel *shame*, it is time to find a different perspective. If you really deserve the feeling of shame, change the behavior and let it go. If not, change your thinking by replacing the word shame with the word *perception*. Look for a new perception. The essence of PERCEPTION is to trust your inner knowledge through the channel of healthy discrimination which allows order and self-discipline. In other words, it takes a new perception or consciousness to accurately evaluate a situation and make new decisions even at the level of thoughts.

Instead of *blame, evaluate*. Blame and evaluate have the same energies except blame is negative and evaluate is positive. Blame places responsibility indiscriminately and finds excuses whereas the essence of EVALUATE places responsibility where it really belongs through a broader focus to get to better relationships. You must look at the situation to determine where you are and where you want to go from there. Don't make changes just for the sake of change. You could just complicate the situation more instead of defusing it. For change to be productive, you must think through a plan of action and be prepared for the reactions that may come.

To make this tool work for you, you need to do some mind/energy work. By that I mean you need to form a habit of using positive connotation words. A good way to do that is to read short statements that focus on what you want to accomplish. Write out a list of phrases or sentences and begin to work with them every day. An example would be "I am learning to be a good decision maker." "I am taking responsibility for my thoughts and actions." "I am good at _____ (fill in the blank)." "I can make good choices." "I love myself." "I am starting to heal." Read poetry. Read uplifting books. Hug a tree. Find the beauty in nature. Find the beauty in people. Listen to inspiring music like the Brandenburg Concertos and Handel's water music for clear thinking and Elgar's Pomp and Circumstance to strengthen your courage. Learn to meditate. Learn to say no when it is appropriate. Focus on the good in things and events. You will find that the first step you take is the hardest in forming new habits. Be persistent. Be consistent. Don't give up.

There is a line in the Cayce material that says to do what you know to do and more will be given. It takes twenty-one consecutive days to establish a habit. If you miss a day, you have to start over with your count. Just as your situation did not happen overnight, the solution will not happen overnight. However, you and I know that when you fail you can start again. It will be easier the second time because you have already introduced a positive pattern. There is a residue on which to build. Don't let one or two or ten failures stop the chain-breaking process, the healing process. Instead, do something kind for someone else, even if it is only a smile. You never know what that smile can mean to someone who is also struggling with change. Be persistent and before long you will see a difference. You will see a shift in your perspective. You will feel better about yourself. These changes give you power to continue the process.

We are hard-wired to want acceptance and support from others. We are hard-wired to want love. Kindness feeds the soul. Love, even self-love, feeds the soul. Kindness and love neutralize negative patterns eventually. If that love is toxic or misused, it begins to tear down the system to which it is directed. If that love is selfless, it is powerful and healing.

Now it's your turn to play with words, your turn to reveal the energy around you. Enjoy your new tool. Begin to think of yourself as someone worthy of love, someone special because that is exactly who you are. There is nothing stronger than you and unconditional love. Claim your healing! Claim your independence! Claim your power!   (See Figure 2 below).

NOTES

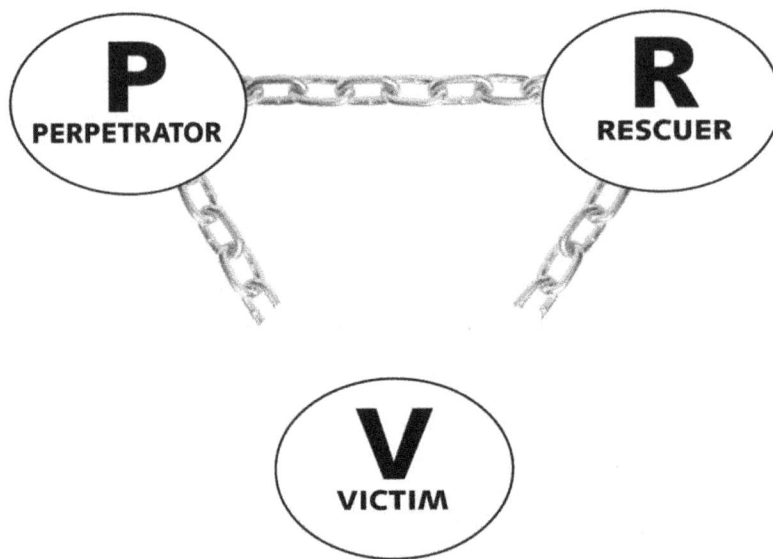

Independence

Figure 2

SOMETHING TO THINK ABOUT

How did you feel as you were reading the first part of this book? I suspect you felt down and a bit depressed whether or not you would describe yourself as a victim. I suspect you noticed there were quite a number of negative words used. It was done deliberately to demonstrate the power of words. The positive words of the chapter, A Way Out, probably gave you a lift in spirit. The words we use impact us as much as the words we hear. Our thoughts impact us as much as others' thoughts being directed at us. It is the vibrations of the spoken word and the thoughts that make the impact. To begin the process of breaking the chains of victimization, we must first take control of our thoughts and/or our moods.

How do we change our mood if we don't like the mood we are in? There are a number of ways to shift our mood. One way is to use color; color therapy can be done in so many ways. Every time we see a color we are getting a treatment. To effect change, we can change the colors we have been observing or shift our focus to a more desirable color. Work with the lighter, cheerier shades rather than the darker, muted shades. Wear different colors, or use new accents in your private space. Visualize a cloud of sunny yellow or beautiful pink surrounding you. Eating specific foods will bring a specific vibration into your energy field. For instance, if you want to have more red in your energy field, eat watermelon, strawberries, tart cherries, red raspberries, or red bell peppers. Eat oranges or carrots for the orange vibration. Lettuce, broccoli, spinach and kale provide the green vibration. Color breathing is another method of color therapy whereby you visualize color and breathe it into your body and direct it to a desired place. There are a number of good color therapy books available to help in using this method for mood changes. The basis of color therapy is vibration. Using a higher vibratory rate will lift a lower vibratory rate. It works just as well when there is a need to tone down a very high vibratory rate.

Another way to change our mood is to use music. Here again we are working with vibrations to bring about change. The Edgar Cayce material states that music is a tool to bridge states of consciousness. Corinne Heline says almost the same thing in her book, <u>Color and Music in The New Age</u>. Pay attention to what music lifts you and what music doesn't. Hal A. Lingerman gives lists of music to use for specific purposes in his book, <u>Healing Energies of Music</u>. He suggests strong music for airing out anger and quiet music to calm anger. According to Lingerman, Copland's *Suite of Old American Songs* and *Battle Hymn of the Republic* will boost strength and courage. Lingerman also states that Johnny Cash's songs reveal the desire for freedom and the desire of the heart to overcome confinements and find love. It is good music to play when we face challenges and when we wish to release our emotions and change our mood. The recommendation most pertinent to this book is to use the brass sounds and cymbals to energize the body especially when we tend to feel a bit sorry for ourselves.

Fragrances can also be powerful mood changers. Perfume is a huge business that takes advantage of the concept. Perfume makers take into consideration the personal vibrations and preferences. Perfumes evoke different impressions when used by different people, otherwise there would be a single scent to attract love. However, scent is not limited to perfumes and colognes. Foods, candles, and chemicals are just a few things that can really change our mood. The food industry is another industry taking full advantage of this concept, knowing that good smelling food changes the mood by starting the digestive process, which results in one feeling hungry. Scents can also provoke flashbacks to previous times that are deeply imbedded in the memory. Scents, in the form of incense used in religious ceremonies, can trigger a feeling of devotion to the Spirit.

Vigilance is necessary when we find ourselves in a depressed state or in a bad mood. What words have we been using? What words have others said that made us begin to withdraw? What kind of music have we been hearing? What have our color choices been lately? Once these questions are answered, we have an idea of how we can begin to change our feelings.

As you can see, we have been given five means for detecting vibrations. We use the senses of touch, taste, smell, hearing and sight to decode the information received through vibrations. Our body uses these impressions to understand the world in which we live. If we are constantly bombarded with vibrations, why not use them to accomplish what we want, to create a healthy environment for our safety and enjoyment? Focus on what you want and how you want to feel, not on how bad the world is. When you focus on how bad the world is, you are adding to the negative energy. You are keeping it alive and well. Change your thoughts and help dissipate the negative energies that may surround you so the healing process can be accelerated. There is so much beauty in this world if you can open your eyes and find it. Once you begin the process, you will draw the help you need. Each step will be a bit easier thereby bolstering your confidence. Remember, the Devine Spark in you is perfect.

Begin to do your own investigation of vibrations. See if these suggestions work for you. Begin to plan the steps you can take to bring you to a healthy and safe place mentally as well as physically. As stated previously, now is the time for you to break the links binding you to pain. Now is the time to claim your empowerment. Now is the time to be who you want to be.

NOTES

WORD LIST

The following section is a listing of words, the connotation of the idea conveyed by the words, as well as the numbers revealed when applying the system of numerology. A brief interpretation of the energy of the words is included.

Abuse ~ negative ~ 9, 3, 3 ~ lack of healing through destruction of joy to lack of self-confidence

Abused ~ negative ~ 9, 7, 7 ~ lack of healing through misuse of wisdom to poor self-image

Acceptance ~ neutral ~ 3, 5, 8 – joy through change to power

Accomplish ~ positive ~ 7, 11, 9 ~ better self-image through challenge to healing

Accomplishment ~ 3, 4, 7 ~ joy through discipline to better self-image

Act ~ positive ~ 1, 5, 6 ~ new beginning through change to taking responsibility for action

Action ~ positive ~ 7, 1, 8 ~ renewed trust through action to power

Adopt ~ positive ~ 7, 4, 2 ~ trust inner knowledge through self-discipline to balance

Advantage ~ neutral ~ 8, 22, 3 ~ power through step by step building to confidence

Attacked ~ negative ~ 7, 4, 2 ~ poor self-image through lack of self-discipline to imbalance, troublemaker

Attract ~ neutral ~ 2, 9, 2 ~ balance through healing to cooperation

Attracted ~ positive ~ 7, 22, 11 ~ trusting inner strength through step by step building to enlightenment

Awake ~ positive ~ 7, 7, 5 ~ trust inner knowledge through better self-concept to change

Awareness ~ positive ~ 3, 3, 33 ~ joy through confidence to higher level of love

Balance ~ positive ~ 7, 4, 2 ~ better self-concept through self-discipline to peace

Begin ~ positive ~ 5, 5, 1 ~ action through change to new beginning

Beginning ~ positive ~ 5, 4, 9 ~ change through self-discipline to healing and completion

Believe ~ positive ~ 6, 9, 33 ~ service through healing to higher level of love

Bitterness ~ negative ~ 1, 22, 5 ~ lack of new thought through step by step building to lack of freedom

Blame ~ negative ~ 6, 9, 6 ~ undeserved responsibilities or forced service through compassionless intolerance to unbalanced relationships

Boundary ~ neutral ~ 8, 2, 1 ~ power through balance to new beginning

Break ~ neutral ~ 6, 4, 1 ~ taking responsibility through self-discipline to new beginning

Breakthrough ~ positive ~ 6, 11, 8 ~ taking responsibility through challenge to power

Challenge ~ neutral ~ 11, 11, 4 ~ enlightenment through testing to self-discipline

Change ~ neutral ~ 6, 5, 11 ~ responsibility though action to enlightenment and challenge

Children ~ neutral ~ 5, 5, 1 ~ change through restlessness to independence

Choose ~ neutral ~ 8, 3, 11 ~ using higher power through creativity to enlightenment and challenge

Color ~ positive ~ 3, 6, 9 ~ creativity through responsible relationships to healing

Confess ~ neutral ~ 11, 7, 9 ~ enlightenment though trust to healing

Consequence ~ neutral ~ 6, 7, 4 ~ responsibility through trusting inner knowledge to discipline and order

Control ~ neutral ~ 3, 22, 7 ~ joy through step by step building to wisdom

Control ~ negative ~ 3, 22, 7 ~ lack of confidence or joy through building step by step to lack of trust or closing in on self

Create ~ positive ~ 11, 5, 7 ~ challenge through action to trust inner knowledge

Courage ~ positive ~ 6, 1, 7 ~ taking responsibility through new beginning to better self-image

Decision ~ positive ~ 11, 4, 6 ~ challenge and enlightenment through self-discipline to taking responsibility

Defective ~ negative ~ 6, 1, 7 ~ unable to serve through faulty beginning to lack of trust

Degrading ~ negative ~ 6, 9, 6 ~ negative relationships through lack of healing to lack of purpose

Desire ~ positive ~ 1, 5, 6 ~ new beginning through change to responsibility

Determination ~ positive ~ 8, 4, 3 ~ power through organization to confidence

Detour ~ positive ~ 5, 6, 11 ~ change through serving a purpose to enlightenment and challenge

Emotion ~ neutral ~ 8, 11, 1 ~ power through enlightenment to new beginning

Empower ~ positive ~ 7, 7, 5 ~ trusting inner knowledge through better self-image to freedom

Evaluate ~ positive ~ 6, 9, 6 ~ responsibility through broader focus to better relationships

Family ~ positive ~ 8, 4, 3 ~ power through order to joy

Focus ~ neutral ~ 9, 1, 1 ~ discrimination and healing through leadership to new beginning

Forgive ~ positive ~ 2, 8, 1 ~ balance through power to new beginning

Forgiveness ~ positive ~ 7, 33, 4 ~ improved self-image though imaginative discrimination to self-discipline and order

Friend ~ positive ~ 5, 6, 11 ~ change through taking responsibility to enlightenment

Fun ~ positive ~ 3, 11, 5 ~ joy and self-confidence through challenge and enlightenment to freedom

Future ~ neutral ~ 11, 8, 1 ~ enlightenment through bringing spirit into material to new beginning

Grace ~ positive ~ 6, 1, 7 ~ take responsibility though new beginnings to trusting inner wisdom

Gratitude ~ positive ~ 9, 6, 6 ~ healing through responsibility to better relationships

Guilt ~ negative ~ 3, 3, 6 ~ lack of joy through lack of self-confidence to undeserved responsibility

Gullible ~ negative ~ 8, 9, 8 ~ lack of strong will through lack of healing to lack of power

Heal ~ positive ~ 6, 11, 8 ~ responsibility through challenge to recovery of power

Healthy ~ positive ~ 4, 3, 7 ~ order through confidence to better self-image

Hope ~ positive ~ 11, 6, 8 ~ challenge and enlightenment through taking responsibility to power

Humor ~ positive ~ 9, 3, 3 ~ healing through confidence to joy

Ignorant ~ negative ~ 7, 1, 44 ~ lack of trust through difficulty with new beginnings to lack of common sense

Imagination ~ positive ~ 8, 5, 4 ~ power through change to organization

Inspiring ~ positive ~ 9, 7, 7 ~ healing through trusting inner knowledge to better self-concept

Intention ~ positive ~ 11, 1, 3 ~ challenge through new beginning to joy

Joy ~ positive ~ 4, 1, 5 ~ discipline through new beginnings to change

Kindness ~ positive ~ 5, 9, 5 ~ change through healing to freedom

Knowledge ~ positive ~ 7, 8, 6 ~ Trust inner wisdom through proper use of power to better relationships

Laughter ~ positive ~ 9, 11, 11 ~ healing through challenge to enlightenment

Learn ~ positive ~ 6, 8, 5 ~ responsibility through power to change

Learning ~ positive ~ 6, 11, 44 ~ responsibility through challenge to power of strength and courage

Listen ~ neutral ~ 5, 11, 7 ~ change through challenge to trusting inner knowledge

Look ~ neutral ~ 3, 5, 8 ~ joy through change to proper use of power

Looking ~ neutral ~ 3, 8, 11 ~ joy through proper use of power to enlightenment

Love ~ positive ~ 11, 7, 9 ~ challenge and enlightenment through trusting to healing and completions

Meditate ~ positive ~ 2, 3, 5 ~ understanding through joy to freedom

Message ~ neutral ~ 11, 4, 6 ~ challenge through organization to responsibility

Miracle ~ positive ~ 6, 1, 7 ~ service through new beginnings to inner knowledge

Misery ~ negative ~ 3, 5, 8 ~ lack of joy through lack of change to misuse of power

Motivation ~ neutral ~ 4, 8, 3 ~ organization through exercising the will to confidence

Music ~ positive ~ 3, 8, 2 ~ joy through power of bringing spirit into material to cooperation and peace

Negative ~ negative ~ 2, 9, 11 ~ imbalance through lack of healing to challenge and testing

Non-judgment ~ neutral ~ 1, 33, 7 ~ new beginnings and leadership through higher level of love to healthier self-concept

Open ~ neutral ~ 11, 3, 5 ~ challenge through confidence to freedom

Opportunity ~ positive ~ 4, 5, 9 ~ self-discipline and organization through change to healing and completions

Order ~ neutral ~ 11, 22, 33 ~ challenge through step by step building to higher learning

Overwhelmed ~ negative ~ 3, 1, 4 ~ lack of confidence through lack of new ideas to hard work and lack of organization

Pain ~ negative ~ 1, 3, 22 ~ lack of new beginning through lack of motivation to tearing down step by step

Painful ~ negative ~ 4, 3, 7 ~ lack of discipline though lack of joy to lack of trust, poor image

Past ~ neutral ~ 1, 1, 11 ~ independence through new beginnings to enlightenment

Peace ~ positive ~ 11, 1, 3 ~ enlightenment through new beginnings to joy

Perception ~ neutral ~ 7, 33, 4 ~ going within through higher love to organization and discipline

Perpetrator ~ negative ~ 8, 9, 8 ~ misuse of authority, through lack of healing to misuse of power

Play ~ positive ~ 8, 1, 9 ~ power through new beginning to healing

Positive ~ positive ~ 11, 5, 7 ~ enlightenment though change to wisdom

Power ~ neutral ~ 11, 3, 5 ~ master enlightenment through confidence to change

Powerless ~ negative ~ 7, 8, 6 ~ distrust through control to servant or slavery

Pray ~ positive ~ 8, 7, 6 ~ power of bringing spirit into material through trusting inner strength to better relationships

Prayer ~ positive ~ 4, 7, 11 ~ self-discipline and organization through inner strength to enlightenment

Present ~ neutral ~ 1, 6, 7 ~ new beginning through taking responsibility to trust and better self-concept

Profess ~ neutral ~ 11, 6, 8 ~ enlightenment through service to power

Promise ~ positive ~ 2, 3, 5 ~ balance though confidence to action

Proven ~ positive ~ 11, 7, 9 ~ enlightenment and testing through trusting inner knowledge to healing

Punish ~ negative ~ 3, 3, 33 ~ lack of confidence through lack of joy to failure to protect

Read ~ neutral ~ 6, 4, 1 ~ service through self-discipline to new beginning

React ~ neutral ~ 6, 5, 2 ~ responsibility through change to cooperation

Reaction ~ neutral ~ 3, 1, 4 ~ confidence through new beginning to organization

Release ~ neutral ~ 7, 4, 11 ~ better self-image through discipline to enlightenment

Rescuer ~ neutral ~ 4, 22, 8 ~ organization through building step by step to power

Role ~ neutral ~ 11, 3, 5 ~ challenge through creativity to change

Sabotage ~ negative ~ 4, 3, 7 ~ lack of discipline through lack of joy and creativity to faulty perception and untrustworthiness

Self-discipline ~ positive ~ 1, 33, 7 ~ new beginning through higher learning to trust

Shame ~ negative ~ 6, 4, 1 ~ negative aspects of responsibility through discipline to inability to do anything new

Smile ~ positive ~ 5, 8, 22 ~ change through power to building step by step

Solve ~ positive ~ 11, 8, 1 ~ challenge through power to new beginning

Standard ~ neutral ~ 2, 7, 9 ~ balance though trusting inner knowledge to healing

Start ~ positive ~ 1, 5, 6 ~ new beginning through action to responsibility

Starting ~ positive ~ 1, 8, 9 ~ new beginning through power to healing and completions

Suffer – negative – 8, 22, 3 – misuse of power through step by step action to destruction of joy and creativity

Suicidal ~ negative ~ 22, 11, 33 ~ tearing down step by step though challenge to lack of higher learning

Survive ~ positive ~ 8, 9, 8 ~ bringing spirit into material through healing to power

Survivor ~ positive ~ 9, 9, 9 ~ tolerance through completions to healing

Teach ~ neutral ~ 6, 4, 1 ~ responsibility through discipline and order to new understanding

Think ~ neutral ~ 9, 8, 8, ~ healing through proper use of power to empowerment

Thinking ~ neutral ~ 9, 11, 11 ~ healing through challenge to enlightenment

Tool ~ neutral ~ 3, 5, 8 ~ creativity through change to proper use of power

Toxic ~ negative ~ 6, 11, 8 ~ taking undue responsibility through challenge to misuse of power

Treatment ~ positive ~ 11, 6, 8 ~ creativity through responsibility to empowerment

Trust ~ positive ~ 3, 5, 8 ~ joy through freedom to power

Tunnel vision ~ negative ~ 5, 7, 3 ~ lack of change through mistrust to lack of confidence

Unlovable ~ negative ~ 6, 8, 5 ~ unsuccessful relationships through misuse of power to resisting change

Useless ~ negative ~ 4, 6, 1 ~ lack of self-discipline through service or servitude to failure to find solutions and new beginnings

Valuable ~ positive ~ 1, 3, 22 ~ new beginnings through creativity to step by step building

Victim ~ negative ~ 9, 4, 4 ~ lack of healing through lack of discipline to disorientation

Withdrawal ~ negative ~ 11, 9, 11 ~ lack of meeting a challenge through non-completion to testing

Wonder ~ neutral ~ 11, 5, 7 ~ enlightenment through action to trust

Work ~ neutral ~ 6, 7, 22 ~ responsibility through inner strength to building step by step

NOTES

LETTER VALUE CHART

Value	1	2	3	4	5	6	7	8	9
Letter	A	B	C	D	E	F	G	H	I
Letter	J	K	L	M	N	O	P	Q	R
Letter	S	T	U	V	W	X	Y	Z	

NUMBER COMPONET CHART

Value 1 (A, J, S)	Value 2 (B, K, T)	Value 3 (C, L, U)
Red	Orange	Yellow
Ruby, Red Garnet	Moonstone	Yellow Topaz
Musical Note/Key 'C'	Musical Note/Key 'D'	Musical Note/Key "'E'
New, Leader, Independent	Balance, Cooperation, Peace	Joy, Self-confidence, Creative
Value 4 (D, M, V)	**Value 5 (E, N, W)**	**Value 6 (F, O, X)**
Green	Blue	Indigo
Emerald, Green Jade	Turquoise, Aquamarine	Pearls, Blue Sapphire
Musical Note/Key 'F'	Musical Note/Key 'G'	Musical Note/Key 'A'
Discipline, Organize, Hard Work	Change, Freedom, Sensuous	Relationships, Responsibility
Value 7 (G,P,Y)	**Value 8 (H, Q, Z)**	**Value 9 (I,R)**
Violet	Pink, Fuchsia	All colors, White
Amethyst	Diamond, Pink Quartz	Opal
Musical Note/Key 'B'	Musical Note/Key 'High C'	Musical Note/Key 'High D'
Trust wisdom, Self-image	Power, Boss, Spirit into material	Healing, Completions, Tolerance

EXAMPLES

Word	H	E	A	L	I	N	G				
Vowels		5	1		9			5+1+9=15; 1+5=6		Essence	6
Consonants	8			3		5	7		8+3+5+7 = 23 2+3 = 5		Channel	5
All Letters	8	5	1	3	9	5	7		8+5+1+3+9+5+7 = 38, 3+8 = 11		Message 11

Word	H	E	A	L	T	H	Y				
Vowels		5	1				7	5+1+7 = 13 1+3 = 4		Essence	4
Consonants	8			3	2	8		8+3+2+8 = 21 2+1 = 3		Channel	3
All Letters	8	5	1	3	2	8	7	8+5+1+3+2+8+7 = 34, 3+4 = 7		Message 7

Word	H	A	P	P	Y						
Vowels		1			7			1+7 = 8		Essence	8
Consonants	8		7	7				8+7+7 = 22		Channel	22
All Letters	8	1	7	7	7			8+1+7+7+7 = 30, 3+0 = 3		Message	3

Word	H	O	P	E							
Vowels		6		5				6+5 = 11		Essence	11
Consonants	8		7					8+7 = 15 1+5=6		Channel	6
All Letters	8	6	7	5				8+6+7+5 = 26, 2+6 = 8		Message	8

WORKSHEET

Word											
Vowels										Essence	
Consonants										Channel	
All Letters										Message	

Word											
Vowels										Essence	
Consonants										Channel	
All Letters										Message	

Word											
Vowels										Essence	
Consonants										Channel	
All Letters										Message	

Word											
Vowels										Essence	
Consonants										Channel	
All Letters										Message	

www.ingramcontent.com/pod-product-compliance
Lightning Source LLC
Chambersburg PA
CBHW081545040426
42448CB00015B/3231